# Let There Be Light

## BIBLE STORIES

### illustrated by

## JANE RAY

Dutton Children's Books • New York

FOR IAN, MARGOT, ELEANOR, JOHN AND SOPHIE LAWRENCE

WITH LOVE

*J.R.*

The words from the Book of Genesis and the Gospels of Matthew and Luke have been taken
from the Authorized King James Version of the Bible.

Copyright © 1990, 1991, 1992 by Jane Ray
All rights reserved.
CIP Data is available.
First published in the United States 1997 by
Dutton Children's Books,
a member of Penguin Putnam Inc.
375 Hudson Street, New York, New York 10014

Originally published in Great Britain 1997 by Orchard Books, London
Typography by Semadar Megged
Printed in Singapore    First American Edition
3 5 7 9 10 8 6 4 2
ISBN 0-525-45925-1

THE STORY OF THE

Creation

Noah's Ark

THE STORY OF Christmas

# THE STORY OF THE
# Creation

This is a story of how the world began.

And the earth was without form, and void; and darkness was upon the face of the deep.

And the Spirit of God moved upon the waters. And God said, Let there be light: and there was light.

And God saw the light, that it was good: and God divided the light from the darkness. And God called the light Day, and the darkness he called Night. And the evening and the morning were the first day.

DAY

NIGHT

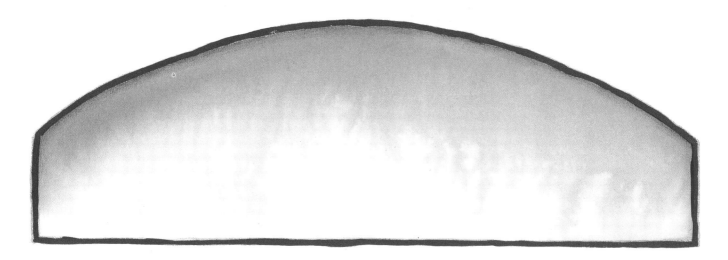

And God said, Let there be a firmament in the midst of the waters, and God made the firmament, and divided the waters. And God called the firmament Heaven. And the evening and the morning were the second day.

And God said, Let the waters under the heaven be gathered together unto one place, and let the dry land appear: and it was so.

And God called the dry land Earth; and the gathering together of the waters called he Seas: and God saw that it was good.

And God said, Let the earth bring forth grass, the herb yielding seed, and
the fruit tree yielding fruit after its kind upon the earth: and it was so.

And the earth brought forth grass, and herb yielding seed after its kind,
and the tree yielding fruit after its kind: and God saw that it was good.
And the evening and the morning were the third day.

| MARCH | APRIL | MAY | JUNE | JULY | AUGUST |

SPRING

SUMMER

And God said, Let there be lights in the firmament of the heaven to divide
the day from the night; and let them be for seasons, and for days, and
years. And God made two great lights; the greater light to rule the day,
and the lesser light to rule the night: he made the stars also.

SEPTEMBER OCTOBER NOVEMBER DECEMBER JANUARY FEBRUARY

FALL

WINTER

And God set them in the firmament of the heaven to give light upon the earth, and to rule over the day and over the night, and to divide the light from the darkness: and God saw that it was good. And the evening and the morning were the fourth day.

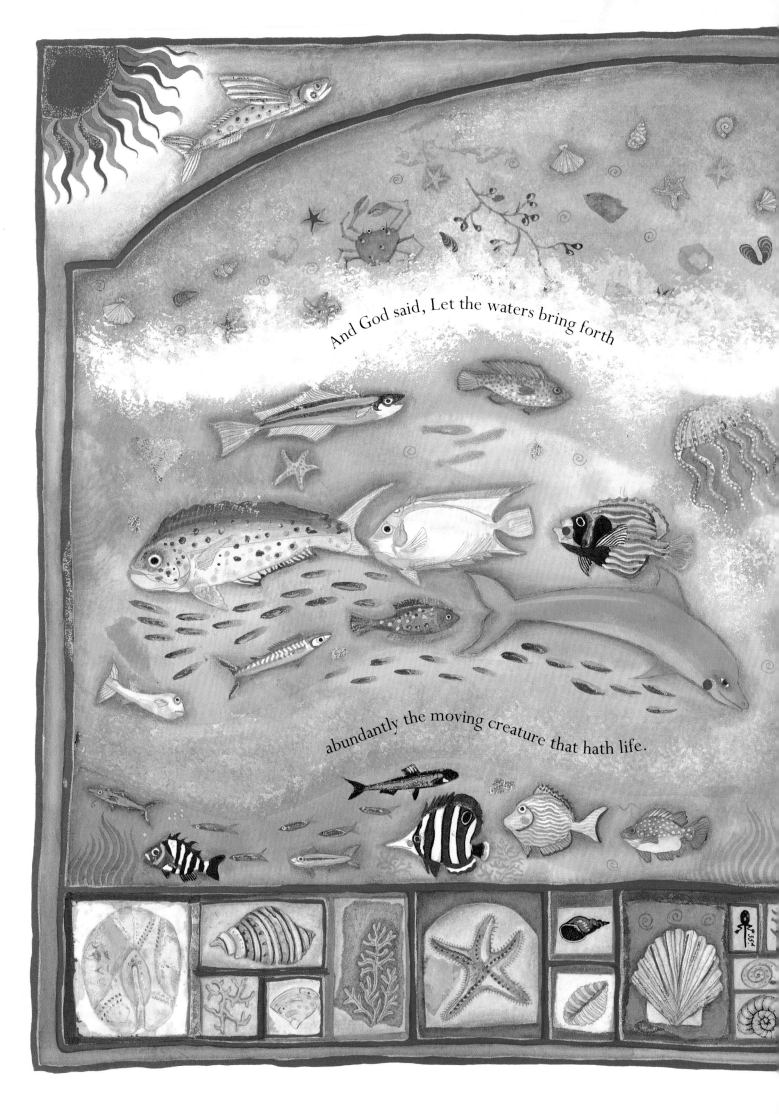

And God said, Let the waters bring forth

abundantly the moving creature that hath life.

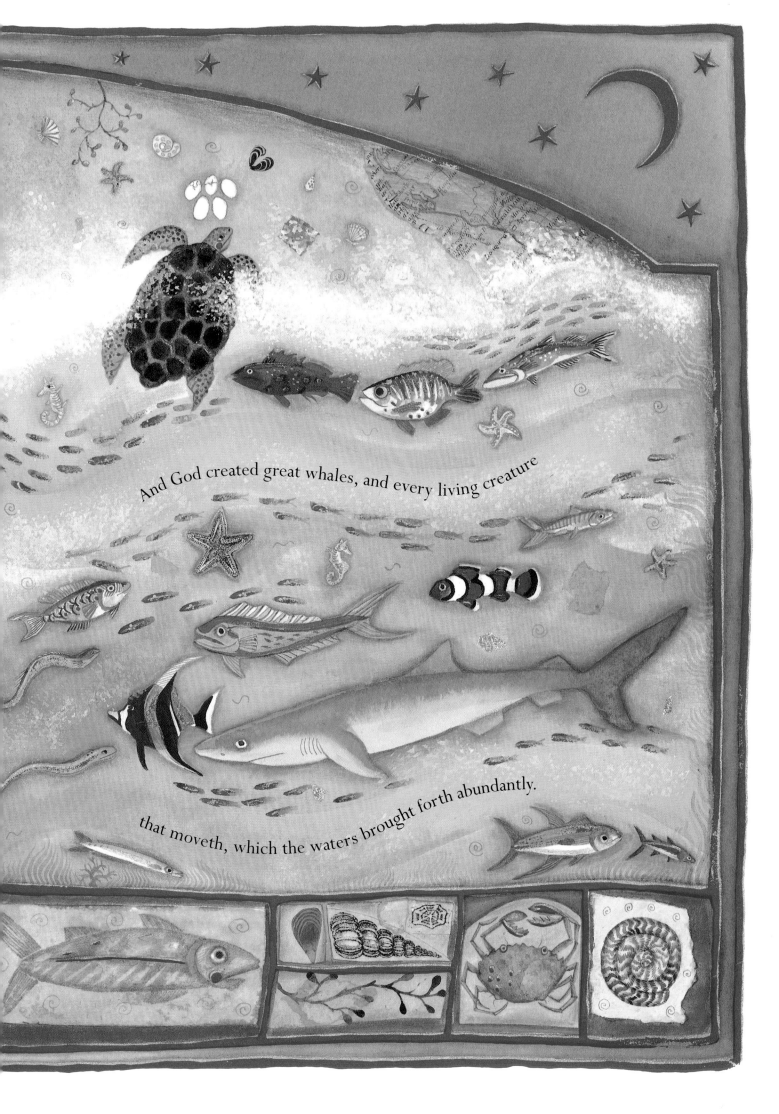

And God created great whales, and every living creature that moveth, which the waters brought forth abundantly.

And God saw that it was good. And God blessed them, saying, Be fruitful, and multiply, and fill the waters in the seas.

And God said, Let there be fowl that may fly above the earth in the open firmament of heaven.

And God created every winged fowl after its kind:

and God saw that it was good. And God blessed them,

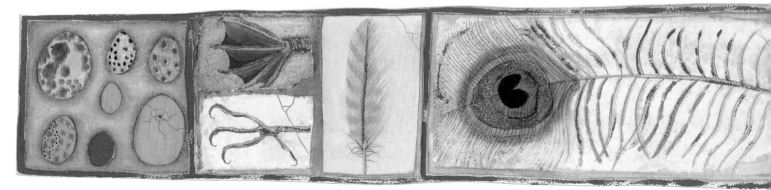

saying, Let fowl multiply in the earth.

And the evening and the morning were the fifth day.

And God said, Let the earth bring forth

the living creature after its kind,

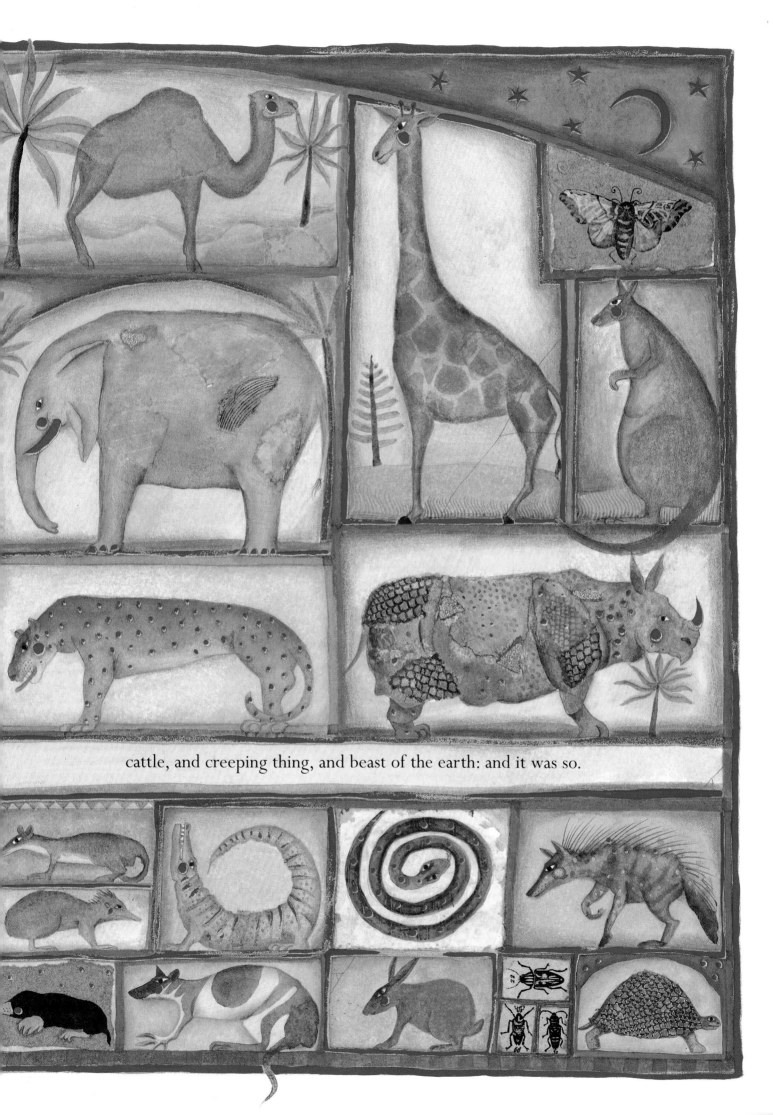

cattle, and creeping thing, and beast of the earth: and it was so.

And God made the beast of the earth after its kind, and cattle after their kind, and every thing that creepeth upon the earth after its kind.

And God saw that it was good.

And God said, Let us make man and woman in our image, after our likeness: and let them have dominion over the fish of the sea, and over the fowl of the air, and over the cattle, and over all the earth, and over every creeping thing that creepeth upon the earth.

So God created humankind in his own image; male and female
created he them.

And God blessed them, and God said unto them, Be fruitful, and multiply, and replenish the earth; and have dominion over every living thing that moveth upon the earth.

And God saw every thing that he had made, and, behold, it was very good.
And the evening and the morning were the sixth day.

Thus the heavens and the earth were finished, and all the host of them.
And on the seventh day God ended his work which he had made;
and he rested.

And that is a story of how the world began.

# Noah's Ark

God saw that the wickedness of man was great in the earth,
and it grieved him at his heart.

And the Lord said, I will destroy man, and beast, and the creeping thing,
and the fowls of the air; for it repenteth me that I have made them.

But Noah found grace in the eyes of the Lord. Noah was a just man, and walked with God. And Noah begat three sons, Shem, Ham, and Japheth.

And God said unto Noah, I will cause it to rain upon the earth forty days and forty nights; and every thing that is in the earth shall die. But with thee will I establish my covenant.

Make thee an ark of gopher wood. Rooms shalt thou make in the ark, and shalt pitch it within and without with pitch. The length of the ark shall be three hundred cubits, the breadth of it fifty cubits, and the height of it thirty cubits.

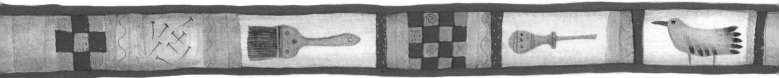

A window shalt thou make to the ark; and the door of the ark shalt thou set in the side thereof; with lower, second, and third stories shalt thou make it.

And thou shalt come into the ark, thou, and thy sons,

and thy wife, and thy sons' wives with thee.

And of every living thing of all flesh, two of every sort shalt thou bring
into the ark,

to keep them alive with thee; they shall be male and female.

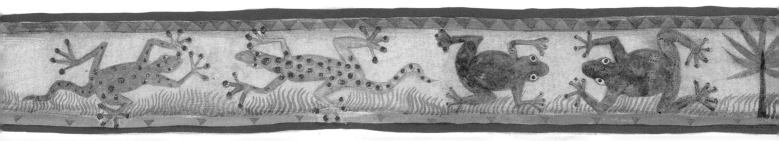

Of fowls of the air

and of beasts, and of every thing

that creepeth upon the earth.

And take thou unto thee of all food that is eaten; and it shall be for
food for thee, and for them. Thus did Noah, according to all that God
commanded him.

And it came to pass after seven days, that the waters of the flood were upon the earth. The windows of heaven were opened; and the ark went upon the face of the waters.

And all the high hills, that were under the whole heaven, were covered.

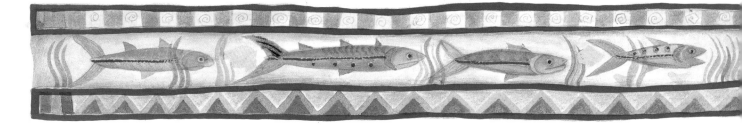

And the mountains were covered.

Every living substance was destroyed which was upon the ground, both man, and cattle, and the creeping things, and the fowl of the heaven;

and Noah only remained alive, and they that were with him in the ark.

And God remembered Noah, and made a wind to pass over the earth.
The rain from heaven was restrained, and the ark rested upon the
mountains of Ararat. And the waters decreased continually until the
tops of the mountains were seen.

And at the end of forty days Noah opened the window
of the ark and sent forth a dove,

to see if the waters were abated from off the ground. But she found
no rest for the sole of her foot and returned into the ark.

And again Noah sent forth the dove; and the dove came in to him in the evening; and in her mouth was an olive leaf; so Noah knew that the waters were abated from off the earth. And at the end of seven days Noah again sent forth the dove, which returned not unto him any more.

And Noah removed the covering of the ark, and looked, and, behold, the face of the ground was dry. And God spake unto Noah, saying, I will set my bow in the cloud, and it shall be a token of a covenant between me and you and every living creature.

Go forth of the ark, thou, and thy wife, and thy sons, and thy sons' wives
with thee. Bring forth with thee every living thing that is with thee, both
of fowl, and of cattle, and of every creeping thing that creepeth upon

the earth. Be fruitful, and multiply, and replenish the earth,
for I will not curse the ground any more.

nd while the earth remaineth, seedtime and harvest,
and cold and heat, and summer and winter,
and day and night shall not cease.

# THE STORY OF

# Christmas

$J$n the days of Herod, the king of Judea, there was a virgin espoused to a man named Joseph. She lived in the city of Nazareth, and her name was Mary.

And the angel Gabriel was sent from God unto her, and said, Hail, thou
that art highly favored, the Lord is with thee: blessed art thou among
women. Fear not, for thou shalt bring forth a son, and shalt call his name
Jesus. He shall be great, and shall be called the Son of the Highest;

and of his kingdom there shall be no end. And Mary said, Behold
the handmaid of the Lord; be it unto me according to thy word.
And the angel departed from her.

And it came to pass in those days, that there went out a decree
from Caesar Augustus, that all the world should be taxed.

So all went to be taxed, every one into his own city.

And Joseph also went into Judea, to be taxed

with Mary his espoused wife, being great with child.

And so it was, that, while they were there,
in the city of David, which is called Bethlehem,

the days were accomplished that she should be delivered.

And she brought forth her firstborn son,
and wrapped him in swaddling clothes, and
laid him in a manger; because there was
no room for them in the inn.

And there were in the same country shepherds abiding in the field,
keeping watch over their flock by night. And, lo, the angel of the Lord
came upon them, and the glory of the Lord shone round about them:
and they were sore afraid. And the angel said unto them, Fear not: for,

behold, I bring you good tidings of great joy, which shall be to all people. For unto you is born this day in the city of David a Savior, which is Christ the Lord. And this shall be a sign unto you; Ye shall find the babe wrapped in swaddling clothes, lying in a manger.

And suddenly there was with the angel a multitude
of the heavenly host praising God, and saying,

Glory to God in the highest, and on earth peace, good will toward men.

As the angels were gone away from them into heaven, the shepherds said
one to another, Let us now go even unto Bethlehem, and see this thing

which the Lord hath made known unto us. And they came with haste, and found Mary, and Joseph, and the babe lying in a manger.

And when they had seen it, they made known abroad the saying which was told them concerning this child.

And all they that heard it wondered at those things which were told them
by the shepherds.

Now when Jesus was born in Bethlehem of Judea in the days of Herod the king, behold, there came wise men from the east to Jerusalem, saying,

Where is he that is born King of the Jews? for we have seen his star
in the east, and are come to worship him.

When Herod the king had heard these things, he was troubled, and all Jerusalem with him. Then Herod, when he had privily called the wise men, enquired of them diligently what time the star appeared.

And he sent them to Bethlehem, and said, Go and search diligently for
the young child; and when ye have found him, bring me word again,
that I may come and worship him also.

When they had heard the king, they departed;
and, lo, the star, which they saw in the east,

went before them, till it came and stood over
where the young child was.

And they saw the young child with Mary his mother, and fell down, and worshipped him: and when they had opened their treasures, they presented unto him gifts; gold, and frankincense, and myrrh. And being warned of God that they should not return to Herod, they departed into their own country.

And behold, the angel of the Lord appeareth to Joseph, saying, Arise, and take the young child and his mother, and flee into Egypt: for Herod will seek to destroy him. When he arose, he took the child and his mother, and departed into Egypt.

ut when Herod was dead, Joseph took the young child and his mother, and returned to Nazareth. And the child grew, and waxed strong in spirit: and the grace of God was upon him.

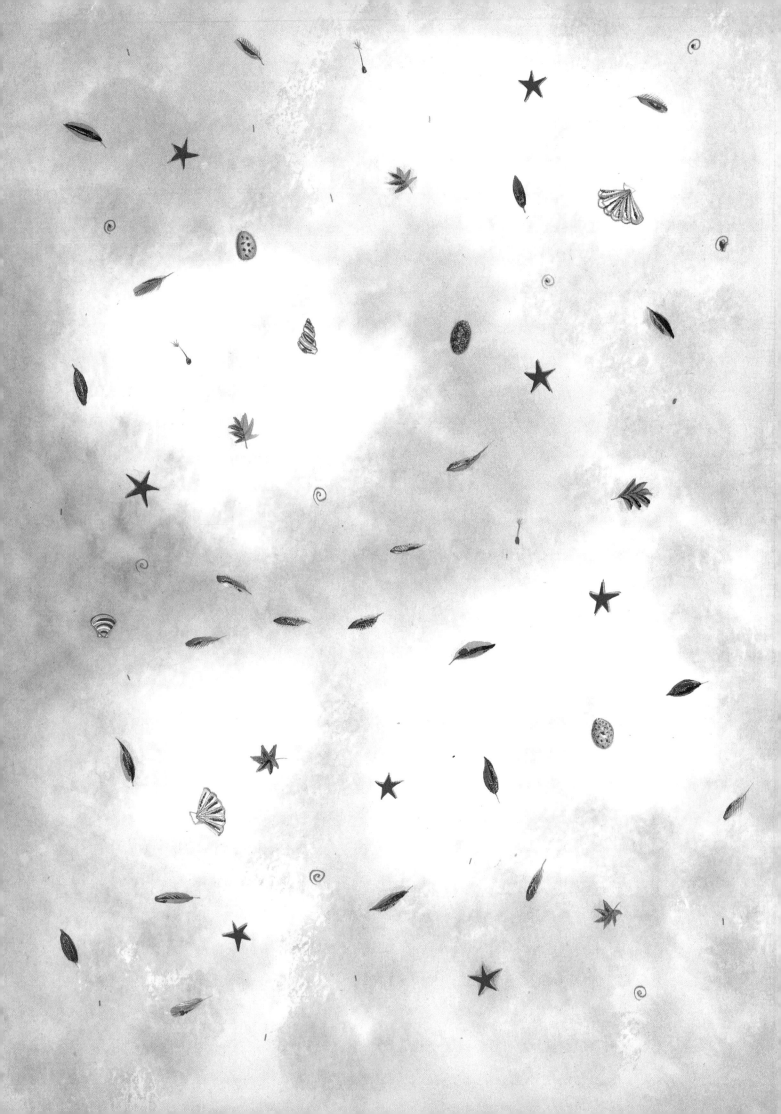